Take The Bullying By The Horns

Take the Bullying by the Horns

Copyright © 2019 by Hunter Dan

All rights reserved. No part of this publication may be reproduced, distributed, or transmitted in any form or by any means, including photocopying, recording, or other electronic or mechanical methods, without the prior written permission of the author, except in the case of brief quotations embodied in critical reviews and certain other noncommercial uses permitted by copyright law.

Paperback   978-1-6455054-0-2

Matchstick Literary
3000 Atrium Way
Suite 200 - PMB 20019
Mt. Laurel, NJ 08054-3910
info@matchliterary.com
www.matchliterary.com

Take The Bullying By The Horns

By Hunter Dan

Illustrations By Pam Hodgdon

I walk to school every day. I like school but lately this older boy named Billy waits for me to walk by and jumps out and makes me give him the sandwich my mom packed for my lunch. I don't like going to school anymore. I can't tell anyone because he said if I do he will beat me up.

This has happened every day for a long time. My mom makes my lunch while I sit at the table and eat my breakfast. Now I wait until she finishes making my lunch and goes upstairs to get ready for work. I sneak back into the kitchen and make another sandwich to hide. When Billy takes my sandwich I have another one hidden in my backpack.

When I get to school I take the one hidden in my backpack and put it in my lunchbox. Now I don't have to go hungry. I went hungry for a really long time.

Today is Thursday and after lunch we have an assembly in the gym. We all went to the gym and sat in the bleachers. Mr. Hingston came out with this man who was really tall dressed in a red, white and blue uniform and stood at center court. Mr. Hingston introduced him as 7 Footer and said," he is on the Harlem Prostars. They are playing in a benefit basketball game here tomorrow night to raise money to replace the bridge that crosses the river to the athletic fields that was destroyed in the hurricane".

Then he handed 7 Footer the microphone. 7 Footer said, " Hello as Mr. Hingston said they call me 7 Footer. I started the Harlem Prostars after several years in the NBA. I played on a few teams and as I got older I found I love comedy basketball. So here I am, does anyone want to learn some tricks with the basketball"? He picked a few kids who raised their hand and they went down on the court. Then he asked a couple of teachers to go down.

7 Footer showed them some trick moves while dribbling the ball. The kids and teachers were trying but they weren't doing very well. It was so funny, we were all laughing.

Then 7 Footer said, " I would like to get serious and talk about some things that you may experience in and around school. Is that ok"?

Do you all get good grades? It's really important to get good grades. If you have a test coming up you have to study for it. If you have a homework assignment make sure you do the homework. If you don't understand an assignment ask a teacher or a parent. If you play sports you have to have passing grades or you can't participate. That is letting your team mates and coaches down. So speak up and get help if you need it ok?

Then he talked to us about drugs and alcohol. How it can hurt us and our families. He said " doing drugs and drinking alcohol is so dangerous for young kids. They will destroy your mind and thought process. They will get you in trouble with the police, the school and your parents.

Then he asked if we knew what bullying was. He said, "bullying is very common in schools. You may know someone who is being bullied, or you may know a bully". All I could think about was what Billy is doing to me. He also said, " bullies can start out with something simple and as they succeed they start demanding more". Is Billy going to ask for more? I thought.

Bullying is wrong and can be stopped. The person being bullied needs to come forward and report it to a parent or a teacher. If you know of someone being bullied you should come forward and tell a parent or a teacher what you know.

In closing 7 Footer said, " don't be a victim. Stand up for yourself, not by confronting the bully but by reporting them. No matter what they tell you it can and will be stopped". Thankyou for coming and I hope you all bring your parents to the game tomorrow night. Have a great rest of your day! Bye guys!

When everyone was gone I went down to Mr. Hingston and 7 Footer and told them what Billy was doing to me. Mr Hingston said," Billy is doing this every day"? Yes, I told him. I will put a stop to it Timmy. Thank you for coming forward, that is very brave of you. Mr Hingston put his hand on my shoulder and said, " I am so proud of you Timmy".

The next morning on my way to school I was hoping Billy wasn't waiting for me, but he was. He jumped out from behind a tree and said, " hand it over". While I was opening my lunchbox Mr Hingston came out of nowhere and said," Billy what are you doing"? Billy was stunned, he couldn't even speak. I know you've been taking Timmy's sandwich every day and I'm here to put a stop to it once and for all. Your coming with me mister! He grabbed ahold of Billy and led him toward school.

When I got to school everything was normal except I never saw Billy. When I got home from school my mom and dad were there waiting for me. They said that Mr. Hingston called and told them what Billy was doing to me and that he will never do it again. They said that if I ever have a problem of any kind I can come to them and we'll work it out. Then they hugged me and said to go get ready for tonight. I said, tonight, what is tonight? Mr. Hingston told us that 7 Footer invited us to the benefit game and he wants you to be his special guest.

We got to the game and it was so amazing. The Prostars are so good and they had us all laughing. 7 Footer had me sitting on their bench all game. All the other kids were envious. I got autographs from the team and even got my picture taken with the whole team.

When my parents and I were saying goodbye, 7 Footer picked me up and gave me a hug. He said," you don't have to be afraid walking to school anymore. You are a role model for all kids everywhere. I am so proud of you Timmy, You took the bullying by the horns".